Dawn McMillan

I have a loose tooth.
Can you see it?

I have a loose tooth.
When will it fall out?

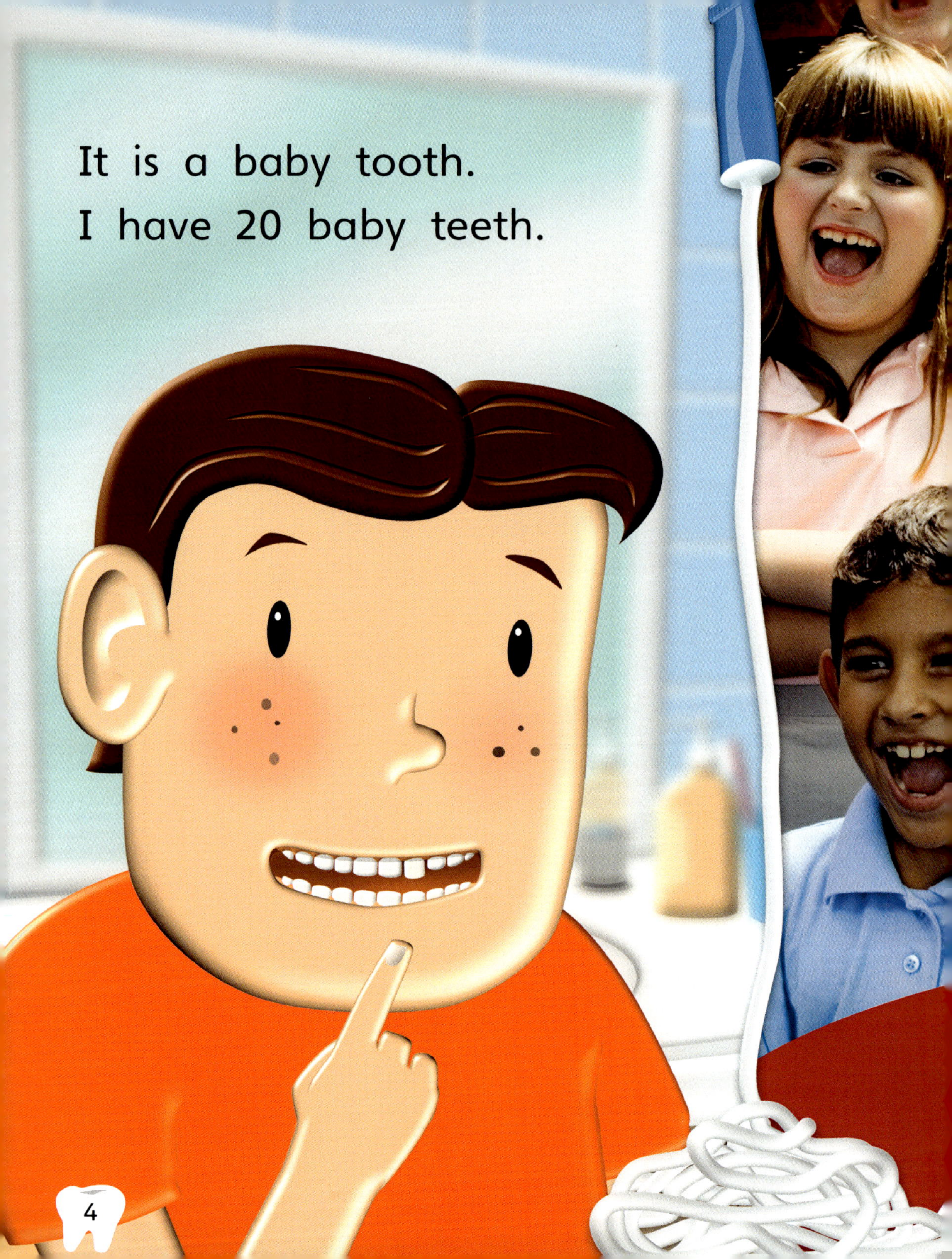

It is a baby tooth.
I have 20 baby teeth.

Babies grow baby teeth.
Babies grow into children.
Then, children grow big teeth.

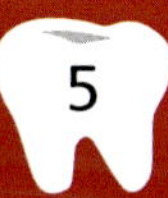

When we are little,
we have little teeth.

When we grow big,
we have bigger teeth!

A big tooth grows in my gum.
I cannot see it.

It will push my baby tooth.
My baby tooth will fall out.

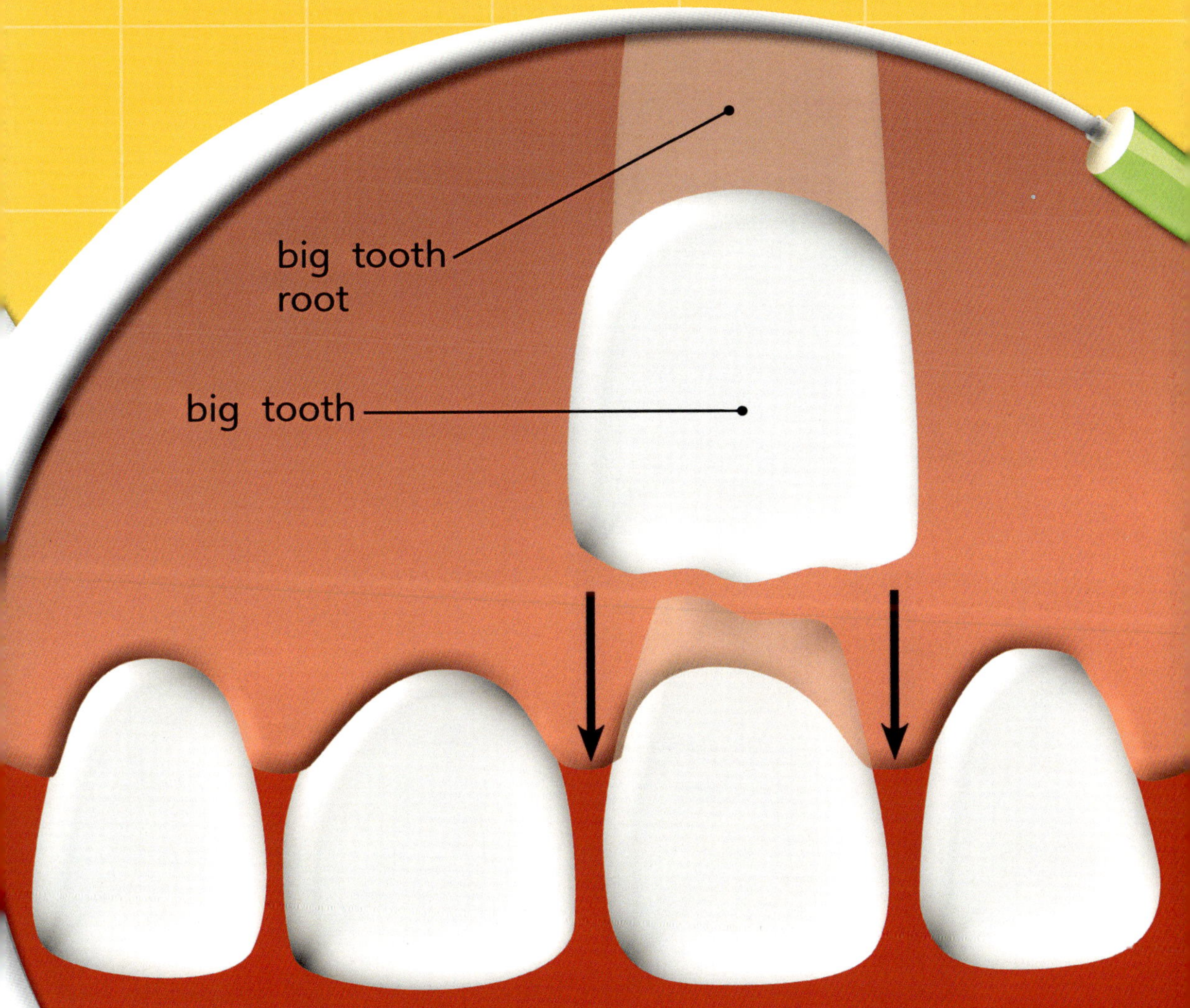

big tooth root

big tooth

My baby tooth will fall out.

It will not hurt
when the tooth falls out.
Then, a big tooth will grow.

You will grow 32 big teeth.
That is a lot of teeth!

Teeth help us eat.
You can eat meat.
Rip!

You can eat fruit.

You can eat vegetables.

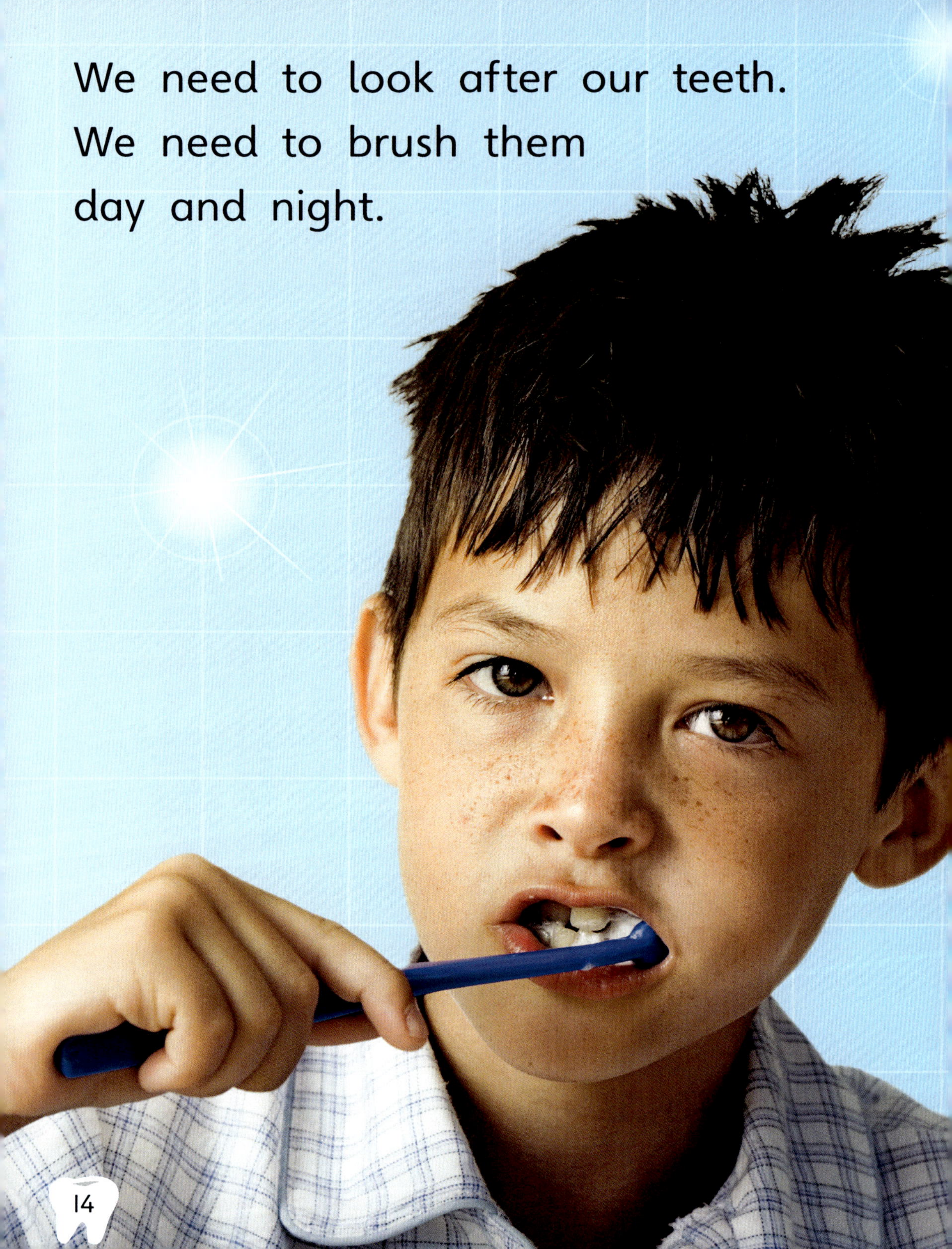

We need to look after our teeth. We need to brush them day and night.

Look!
My loose tooth
fell out!

Here is my tooth.
Good night!